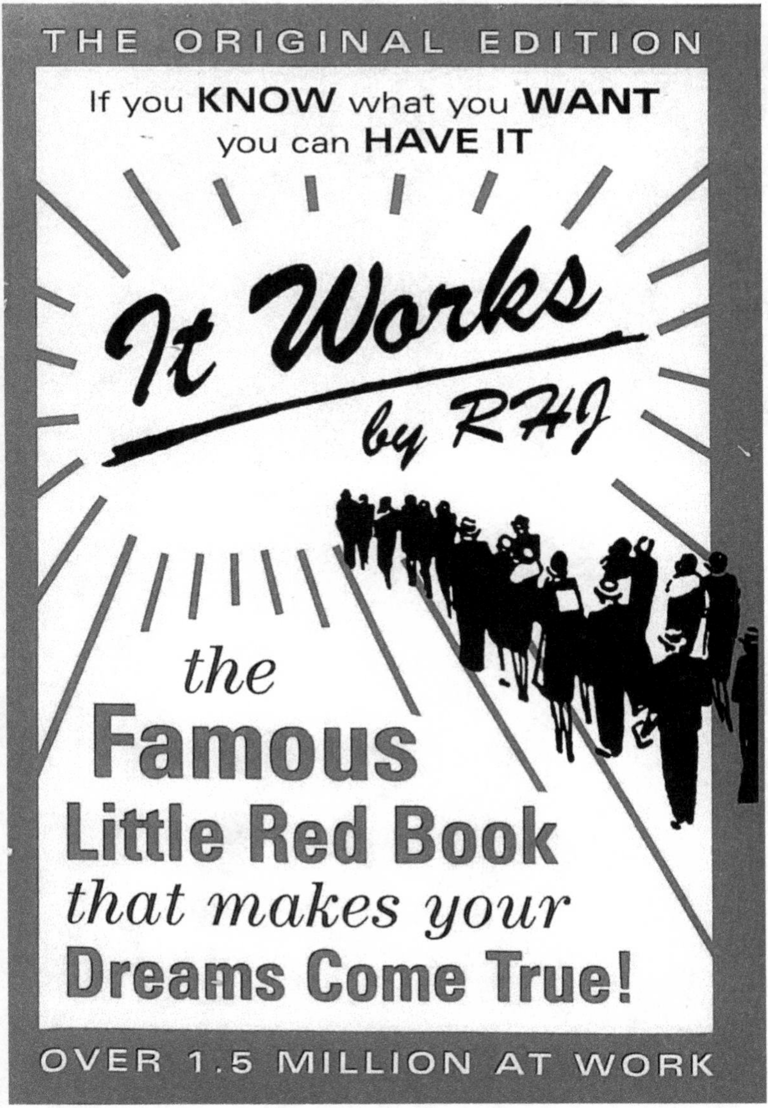
THE ORIGINAL EDITION
If you KNOW what you WANT
you can HAVE IT
It Works
by RHJ
the
Famous
Little Red Book
that makes your
Dreams Come True!
OVER 1.5 MILLION AT WORK

To RHJ

It Works *

JFS

*The author sent the manuscript of this book for criticism to a friend who returned it with the notation, "IT WORKS." This judgment born of experience was adopted as the title of the book.—*Publishers*

This book
with its valuable message
is presented to you
by

_____

It Works

All who joy would win must share it,
Happiness was born a twin.
                                          BYRON

It Works
Copyright © 1926, 1953

Positive Mental Attitude (PMA)

Publishing

www.pmapublishing.com

A concise, definite, resultful plan with rules, explanations and suggstions for bettering your condition in life.

If you KNOW what you WANT you can HAVE IT

The man who wrote this book is highly successful and widely known for his generosity and helpful spirit. He gives full credit for all that he has accomplished in mastering circumstances, accumulating wealth and winning friends to the silent working out of the simple, powerful truth which he tells of in his work. He shows you here an easy, open road to a larger, happier life. Knowing that the greatest good comes from helping others without expecting praise, the author of this work has requested that his name be omitted.

What is the Real Secret of Obtaining Desirable Possessions?

ARE some people born under a lucky star or other charm which enables them to have all that which seems so desirable, and if not, what is the cause of the difference in conditions under which men live?

Many years ago, feeling that there must be a logical answer to this question, I decided to find out, if possible, what it was. I found the answer to my own satisfaction, and for years, have given the information to others who have used it successfully.

From a scientific, psychological or theological viewpoint, some of the

It Works

following statements may be inter-
preted as incorrect, but nevertheless,
the plan has brought the results desired
to those who have followed the simple
instructions, and it is my sincere belief
that I am now presenting it in a way
which will bring happiness and possessions to many more.

'IF wishes were horses, beggars
would ride," is the attitude taken
by the average man and woman in
regard to possessions. They are not
aware of *a power* so near that it is over-
looked; so simple in operation that it is
difficult to conceive; and so sure in
results that it is not made use of con-
sciously, or recognized as *the cause of
failure or success.*

It Works

"GEE, I wish that were mine," is the outburst of Jimmy, the office boy, as a new red roadster goes by; and Florence, the telephone operator, expresses the same thought regarding a ring in the jeweler's window; while poor old Jones, the bookkeeper, during the Sunday stroll, replies to his wife, "Yes, dear, it would be nice to have a home like that, but it is out of the question. We will have to continue to rent." Landem, the salesman, protests that he does all the work, gets the short end of the money and will some day quit his job and find a real one, and President Bondum, in his private sanctorum, voices a bitter tirade against the annual attack of hay-fever.

It Works

At home it is much the same. Last evening, father declared that daughter Mabel was headed straight for disaster, and today, mother's allowance problem and other trying affairs fade into insignificance as she exclaims, "This is the last straw. Robert's school teacher wants to see me this afternoon. His reports are terrible, I know, but I'm late for Bridge now. She'll have to wait until tomorrow." So goes the endless stream of expressions like these from millions of people in all classes who give no thought to what they really want, *and who are getting all they are entitled to or expect.*

If you are one of these millions of thoughtless talkers or wishers and

It Works

would like a decided change from your present condition, you can have it; but first of all you must *know what you want* and this is no easy task. When you can train your *objective mind* (the mind you use every day) to decide definitely upon the things or conditions you desire, you will have taken your first big step in accomplishing or securing what you know you want.

To get what you want is no more mysterious or uncertain than the radio waves all around you. Tune in correctly and you get a perfect result, but to do this, it is, of course, necessary to know something of your equipment and have a plan of operation.

It Works

You have within you a *mighty power*, anxious and willing to serve you, a *power capable* of giving you *that which you earnestly desire*. This power is described by Thomson Jay Hudson, Ph.D., LL.D., author of "The Law of Psychic Phenomena," as your *subjective mind*. Other learned writers use different names and terms, *but all agree that it is omnipotent*. Therefore, I call this Power "Emmanuel" (God in us).

Regardless of the name of this Great Power, or the conscious admission of a God, the Power is *capable and willing* to carry to a complete and perfect conclusion every earnest desire of your objective mind, but you must be really in earnest about what you want.

It Works

Occasional wishing or half-hearted wanting does not form a perfect connection or communication with *your omnipotent power*. You must be in earnest, *sincerely* and *truthfully* desiring certain conditions or things—mental, physical or spiritual.

Your objective mind and will are so vacillating that you usually only WISH for things and the wonderful, capable power within you does not function.

Most wishes are simply vocal expressions. Jimmy, the office boy, gave no thought of possessing the red roadster. Landem, the salesman, was not thinking of any other job or even thinking at all. President Bondum knew he had

It Works

hay fever and was expecting it. Father's business was quite likely successful, and mother no doubt brought home first prize from the Bridge party that day, but they had no fixed idea of what they really wanted their children to accomplish and were actually helping to bring about the unhappy conditions which existed.

If you are in earnest about changing your present condition, here is a *concise, definite, resultful plan, with rules, explanations and suggestions.*

The Plan

WRITE down on paper in order of their importance the things and conditions you really want. Do not be afraid of wanting too much. Go the limit in writing down your wants. Change the list daily, adding to or taking from it, until you have it about right. Do not be discouraged on account of changes, as this is natural. There will always be changes and additions with accomplishments and increasing desires.

Three Positive Rules
Of Accomplishment

1. *Read the list of what you want three times each day: morning, noon and night.*

It Works

2. *Think of what you want as often as possible.*

3. *Do not talk to any one about your plan except to the Great Power within you which will unfold to your Objective Mind the method of accomplishment.*

It is obvious that you cannot acquire faith at the start. Some of your desires, from all practical reasoning, may seem positively unattainable, but, nevertheless, write them down on your list in their proper place of importance to you.

There is no need to analyze how this Power within you is going to accomplish your desires. Such a procedure is

It Works

as unnecessary as trying to figure out why a grain of corn placed in fertile soil shoots up a green stalk, blossoms and produces an ear of corn containing hundreds of grains, each capable of doing what the one grain did. If you will follow this definite plan and carry out the three simple rules, the method of accomplishment will unfold quite as mysteriously as the ear of corn appears on the stalk, and in most cases much sooner than you expect.

When new desires, deserving position at or about the top of your list, come to you, then you may rest assured you are progressing correctly.

Removing from your list items which

It Works

at first you thought you wanted, *is another sure indication of progress.*

It is natural to be skeptical and have doubts, distrust and questionings, but when these thoughts arise, get out your list. Read it over; or if you have it memorized, talk to your inner self about your desires until the doubts that interfere with your progress are gone. *Remember, nothing can prevent your having that which you earnestly desire.* Others have these things. Why not you?

The Omnipotent Power within you does not enter into any controversial argument. *It is waiting and willing to serve when you are ready,* but your

It Works

objective mind is so susceptible to suggestion that it is almost impossible to make any satisfactory progress when surrounded by skeptics. Therefore, choose your friends carefully and associate with people who now have some of the things you really want, but *do not discuss your method of accomplishment with them.*

Put down on your list of wants such material things as money, home, automobile, or whatever it may be, but do not stop there. Be more definite. If you want an automobile, decide *what kind, style, price, color,* and all the other details, including *when* you want it. If you want a home, plan the structure, grounds and furnishings.

It Works

Decide on location and cost. If you want money, write down the amount. If you want to break a record in your business, put it down. It may be a sales record. If so, write out the total, the date required, then the number of items you must sell to make it, also list your prospects and put after each name the sum expected. This may seem very foolish at first, but you can never realize your desires if you do not *know positively and in detail what you want and when you want it.* If you cannot decide this, you are not in earnest. You must be definite, and when you are, results will be surprising and almost unbelievable.

A natural and ancient enemy will no

It Works

doubt appear when you get your first taste of accomplishment. This enemy is Discredit, in form of such thoughts as: "It can't be possible; it just happened to be. What a remarkable coincidence!"

When such thoughts occur *give thanks and assert credit to your Omnipotent Power* for the accomplishment. By doing this, you gain assurance and more accomplishment, and in time, prove to yourself that *there is a law, which actually works—at all times—* when you are in tune with it.

Sincere and earnest thanks cannot be given without gratitude and it is impossible to be thankful and grateful

It Works

without being happy. Therefore, when you are thanking your greatest and best friend, *your Omnipotent Power*, for the gifts received, do so *with all your soul, and let it be reflected in your face*. The Power and what it does is beyond understanding. Do not try to understand it, but *accept the accomplishment* with thankfulness, happiness, and strengthened faith.

Caution

It is possible to want and obtain that which will make you miserable; that which will wreck the happiness of others; that which will cause sickness and death; that which will rob you of eternal life. You can have what you want, but you must take all that goes with it: so in

It Works

planning your wants, *plan that which you are sure will give to you and your fellow man the greatest good here on earth; thus paving the way to that future hope beyond the pale of human understanding.*

This method of securing what you want applies to everything you are capable of desiring and the scope being so great, it is suggested that your first list consist of only those things with which you are quite familiar, such as an amount of money or accomplishment, or the possession of material things. Such desires as these are more easily and quickly obtained than the discontinuance of fixed habits, the welfare of others, and the healing of mental or bodily ills.

It Works

Accomplish the lesser things first. Then take the next step, and when that is accomplished, you will seek the higher and really important objectives in life, but long before you reach this stage of your progress, many worthwhile desires will find their place on your list. One will be to help others as you have been helped. *Great is the reward to those who help and give without thought of self, as it is impossible to be unselfish without gain.*

In Conclusion

A short while ago, Dr. Emil Coué came to this country and showed thousands of people how to help themselves. Thousands of others spoofed at the idea, refused his assistance and are today where they were before his visit.

So with the statements and plan presented to you now. You can reject or accept. You can remain as you are or *have anything you want*. The choice is yours, but God grant that you may find in this short volume the inspiration to choose aright, follow the plan and thereby obtain, as so many others have, all things, whatever they may be, that you desire.

(See next page)

.

It Works

Read the entire book over again, *and again*, AND THEN AGAIN.

Memorize the three simple rules on pages thirteen and fourteen.

Test them now on what you want most *this minute.*

This book could have extended easily over 350 pages, but it has been deliberately shortened to make it as easy as possible for you to read, understand and use. Will you try it? Thousands of bettered lives will testify to the fact that *It Works.*

IT WORKS!
TESTIMONIALS

"Please send another 200 copies of *It Works!*
In answer to your query, yes, we are
obviously using it(!) and yes, we think it's
simply great."

> Carol-Ann Atkinson
> Tri-State Marketing Research
> Overland Park, KS

"*It Works!* has been a proven training
adjunct at Shawmut-Bridges Equities for
almost a decade."

> Kevin Griffin
> Shawmut-Bridges Equities
> Boston, MA

"We now require use of *It Works!* in the first
month of all OAS and OAS Services
training."

> (Lt. Col.) Clark North
> OAS INTEL
> Reston, VA

"Since using *It Works!* in our agent training program, we have noticed a dramatic increase in motivation and performance, and a steady surge in sales that bucks all the downtrends. Please keep it in print."

Stacy York, Vice-President
Pan-Desert Realtors Association
Palm Springs, CA

"I was given *It Works!* in training fourteen years ago and I now require it for training in all Broadmart Centers."

Rick Windsor
Broadmart Sales & Training
San Francisco, CA

"Terrific! Thanks! We've used it for years, and it really *does* work."

Harley Tillman
First Capital Stock & Equity
Silver Springs, MD

A Letter to You
From the Author

Dear Reader:

The great possessions of life are all GIFTS mysteriously bestowed: sight, hearing, aspiration, love or life itself.

The same is true of ideas—the richest of them are given to us, as for instance, the powerful idea which this book has given you. What are you going to do with it? Are you surprised when I tell you the most profitable thing you can do is to give it away?

You can do this in an easy and practical way by having this book sent to those you know who NEED IT. In this way, you can help in the distribution of this worthwhile effort to make the lives of others better and happier.

You know people who are standing still or who are worried and discouraged. This is your chance to HELP THEM HELP THEMSELVES. If you withhold this book from them you will lose the conscious satisfaction that comes from doing good. If you see that they get this book, then you put yourself in line with the Law of Life which says, "You get by giving," and you may rightly expect prosperity and achievement.

At the very least you will have the inner sense of having done a good deed with no hope of being openly thanked and your reward will come secretly in added power and larger life.

THE AUTHOR

(Use order form on next page or write a letter)